The Body Electric Journal

The Body Electric Journal

Paul Lobo Portugés

Plain View Press
P. O. 42255
Austin, TX 78704

plainviewpress.net
sb@plainviewpress.net
1-512-441-2452

Cover photograph: *Eternelle Idole — Variation Lierre*, © 2005,
Mariana Varouta (alias Ina Mar).

Acknowledgments

Some of these poems appeared in: *Ondas, Chelsea, Stonecloud,
Hambone, Alcatraz, Invisible City, Rockbottom, Mudborn Broadside
Press, So Cal, Prufrock, Roof, Ondas, Spectrum, Occasional Review,
Uroboros, Phantasm, Radar, River Styxx, Eye, Le Garleau, Gravida,
Village Idiot, Flute Song, Realities, The Fly, Oberon, Bugle, Hot
Metal*, and other magazines.

Thanks to the Fulbright Commission, the National Endowment,
the Ford Foundation, the Regents of UC, and the Briarcomb
Foundation for help along the way.

Also by Paul Lobo Portugés

Poetry:
*Saving Grace, Hands Across the Earth, Aztec Birth, Paper Song, The
Flower Vendor, Mao* (forthcoming)

Screenplays:
*Jack and Marilyn, Behind the Veil, Pierre, Silent Spring, Fire From the
Mountain, The Body Electric Videos*

Non-fiction:
The Visionary Poetics of Allen Ginsberg
Poetry and Film (forthcoming)

Contents

for the love of my life

Bones of the Sleeping Wind

Above early morning reed tops tiptoe children peer at my long black beard of encouraging thought. Hard work Aztlan songs drift down the crying shore. All day hard luck women pound the long week's laundry just below low flying purple dragonflies over the virgin field of weed covered graves. Half naked boys smack muddy holy water for fat frogs.

In the bitter distance government guns crack and bring everyday everyone to a few seconds still. Sky gazing marguerites wave from the altar bright ridge overlooking the lake of the twelve apostles. Pale deer drink the holy water of slow motion birds crossing the talking waters. Tired living years of race wars I wait for the bride of you in the magenta evening pencil in hand worry watching breaking twilight fade off tuberoses.

I dream you bend your bodyline over the floating moon and drink its cool burning circle. My shadow of manly man folds across your silvered back lust wet with your take me theme of future children golden years and mingled dust. Rivers of blood lift our bones into ritual dance over the witnessing earth. A dark flight of jungle sound passes through our mouth of dreams. We cling together at the foot of a terraced mountain with skeletons of the sleeping wind.

Hot Indian summer late night calls from your oiled jasmine thigh cloud of stark wildness. Red lights blink above the white misty shore our gentle hiss of hips and finally sleeping like cloud warriors.

Staring at Lake Atitlan
I hold your loving
hand of hope
with childlike silence
& never leave

*

I kiss the violin
of your zodiac eyes
sooner and later
in the hand of God willing
we'll be imagined time
heaven driven clouds

*

Washing our altar bodies
near morning's lake bank
we pledge forever vows
though like shooting stars
we fade to black silence

*

Sweat dreamt you
sang forever yours
your diamond lips
opened floating
like waiting arms
and I was here now

*

Midnight opened thighs
wine talking romance
Hiroshima song mystical hip
kisses plus a garden
of porn filled brain
by dawn exhausted
back to forgotten earth
laughter beautiful
tears beautiful

*

Sycamore leaves drift
past tree carved
lovers' hearts near
the overgrown trail

*

Behind kind
weeping walls
a natural woman
a normal man
make love sleep
dream of another

*

Sometimes I can't
tell if I'm you
like our last
screams of night
I you bathing
my your feet

*

She lights
church candles about
our blessed bed
summons private angels
to sleep with
my patriotic rage

*

The crescent moon
my lady painted
with flowers
white moths
beating in the corner

A Media of Loins

Cigarette butts make unusual mosaics in the so-called lawn of the heavily policed park on Mr. Wilshire's boulevard. Gringo kings talk about breeder reactors and beget ribbons of fear in los vatos of the City of Angels. A foot-loose muchacho throws his paper plane past billboards of powdered white pudenda admired by hairless blue blonde never-never-land boys wrestling in surviving dandelions. Across the loud street of modern spirituals lowriders drag their jailed pain screeching past lonely Joe's t.v. repair shop. Booty commercials flash upside down in the smog streaked neon window.

> Brown buffalos
> get English
> in workaday schools
> a meaningful tattoo
> of unforgiving blood
> if they're lucky

> *

> Bullets curse barrio
> poets who eat them
> like dulces then spit
> out histories of pain

> *

> After days of acid
> rain the lost sun
> comes promising
> heaven sent birds
> of children's voices

*

In a vacant lot
a freckled face boy
floats at the happy end
of his 99¢ store kite

*

By corporate t.v. light
media teens
hookup skin deep
with commercial sex
& manufactured want

*

Blood gray light glistens like fool's gold
off polyester suits and pale skinned cor-
ridor serfs hurry-hurrying in a mechanical
vein into glassed-in towers of greed.

The smog heavy sunset spreads volumes of
heated beauty dappling skyscrapers over-
hanging freeway bound money makers on
their sincere way to waiting sighs at night
shift home. Corporate mouths spit on the
unmarked graves of limbless Iraqis and "il-
legal" workers with U.S. steel knives inside
presidential bullshit for lower class help.

Drunk with imagined need
she shops victimized
by highrise multinational
glass & stealing patriots
of plastic cash

*

Honking drivers
shoot me the finger
gonna mess with us;
living the graffiti

*

I cry a witness psalm
a profane river of prayers
when holy bombs
make Satanic tombs
of the sacrificial enemy
asleep in their certain God

*

Original colored skin
gets slave children
beaten innocent souls
on the blue streets
of American pie

*

He sings for his supper
sleeps with fleas
in the manicured bushes
next to the 5 * hotel

*

Bedside guns chemical air
tough living in God bless
America risky if you're
black brown Amerindian
or see with eyes of Asia
or a white woman in the heat
of violent night dicey
even to make love

*

Corporate males undress
hip women passing by
sexualized by pretty
youth bigger & video

*

Knocked down
by skid row
all you want
is cardboard sleep
a clear night
drunken stars

*

After hot weeks
picking shoveling
sleeping in junkyard cars
nos hermanos cross
the imaginary border
to their tossed away lives

*

Day long or star covered
nights good women
walk high heeled
down well lit streets
tired of looking behind

*

Mall teens pretend
they're objects of desire
& with plastic spend
so they can become it

*

But for fortune
homeless rise
in the moist sunrise
from their sleeping ditches
& hunt for a place to shit

*

Smart death bombs
& night-vision soldiers
a good match
against the uprising
of the slow pen

*

Stray bullets
take the innocent
sisters of the street
the brothers' hate
heaped each
upon their other

*

He is an unfortunate
citizen of the corporate needle
a dumpster friend
of alley leftovers
ignored daily
by macho headlines
of little dick wars

*

Go figure
fatherless kids
genocide rape
billion dollar B-2's
larks singing at sunrise

*

He sleeps
in the arms
of those who will
looking for love
until they let him go

*

Yes we fear cloned truths by billboard L.A. and flee
a media of loins that hunts us down in the afternoon
stink of angry-hearted subway voyagers with their
death wish logic and computer ceremonies of deceit.

But with a frail precision of breath we can holy kiss
their torrential reign of nuclear agony and please
stop fighting our modern change all the way to the
trail of tears turned some day to a mime of wild iris.

These it witches waste our sustainable citizenship
with their designer chemicals and tincture of worry
free television. As humans we can sincerely watch
redwinged blackbirds sing a new day awake
and unarmed put on the armor of love cock-
sure of now the gleaming wings of laughter.

The all night
winos stare
at the trashcan
fire warming
their gave you hearts

*

Boys and girls
swagger down
Main St. thinking
they'll live forever

*

Saturday city couples
walk not touching
shop not thinking
brunch talk want to
touch foreheads
then forget

*

Fake tits mean tattoos
do me girls
drink vintage wine
brag about their club lovers

*

Begging for work
or change
she screams
at the sky
about children
she aborted

*

Trampling dazed through an American mutated
breeding ground of nerve loins woven on a violent
nuclear loom of greatness greed worried angels
weep against Sodom's atomic lips of death wish
logic that veils in computer colored light cer-
emonies and in media deceit fragments the grace
filled mourning of long day workers and guilty
managers before pillars of plastic steel dignity.

So we have to please cry love sorrowful love
to gestures of immense dirty dollars and bodies
swollen by interior hunger masculine feminine
cries lost in silver television light soft around the
voiceless twilight of humanity our blood dreaming
eyes morphine slouched into stone military brain.

Singing spirituals
for his supper
he gives me
much more
than the silver dollar
I spare him

*

Laughing and teasing
the boys of summer
swim in the chemical
foam of an old pond

*

The brave soldiers'
drums at rest
just manicured lawns
and head bent lovers
before white crosses

The Wind Falling Into Us

Clutching at woven shadows unraveled in night wind down the back alley of our desperate dream mind our weary bodies fearful after decades of genocide against darker skin. A river of hope races through our trembling limbs while weaving bays silhouette a rising wave upon wave of your early morning breathingthe wind falling into us.

Our backs rise as falling leaves turn to birds at the sight of us. Your sublime brain traces the sides of feeling cuts into my philosophical throat gutted by newspaper worries waiting for the bloom of the war weary world—everything passing into us.

Bodies of broken children scream through our panther heart freed in our natural escape. My nuclear angel come into my electronic outback and free me from the energy wasted bitching streets paved with barrio tears and drugged night loins–all falling into us.

Dawns of shooting stars fill the blood labor of us soothing our crime-ridden thinking inside the lighted nape of your secret moist refuge from steel and children of usury their faces of nip tuck t.v. oh save us from their unnatural machine ragas and daily righteous complaints of one way morality—all passing into us.

Light the light like water falls slow motion over us an incense of Aztlan deep wades through our fire stoned blood siren love of bird song morning afire like you my trembling wildflower shimmering in the wind watch of our secret flying my brother woman breath phantom sister—everything falling into us.

Without you how
could I bear
the wild grasses
on the unkept graves

*

Kill or be killed
the soldier tells us
that's the way it is

*

Fruitless trees
chemical air
bored children
come soon
oh season
of human promises
& ancient rain

*

A prayer for the war's end
for the children's return
to weedy fields
of kites and laughter

*

In the middle of restless night
worried about disease
godless friends terrorists
over electrified Manhattan

*

Bombs hunger lacklove
prodigal sons daughters
abandoned fields
come down God
get to work

*

Sickness war
the scared earth
dead loved ones
janjaweed
the air after rain
there are no words

*

As for our souls
not to worry
they gave us up
when they declared war

*

She was afraid
the swallows
wouldn't come
this spring
what with the war
and all

*

Full of the world
I retreat
sighing dark
between her thighs
I know I'm
fooling myself

The Celebrated Thigh

Above Unreals Beach the cloudy Milky Way.
Acid illumination tears away veils of babble
brain as I hike interior beckoning mountains
of guilty voices to surrender to a blade of grass.
After fear fed weeks sitting past three full
moons utterly alone with my noisy mindfull.

Waves break shattering moon silver and thoughts
about what was it?

So many God stars I too seldom see—stuck in a
world of meat electric distraction the celebrated
thigh. Late spring trade winds of shivering fate
help me surf through personal histories dancing
beyond tits of habit. Temporarily freed my original
sound is quiet seas and everyday fields of strife.

I am bone cold. The blowing kataleya hurt me.

Watching solitary breath
the clouded moon
faraway the starving night

*

Cupping a wood bowl
same size as my belly
eating friendly miso rice

*

In our sad world
I stumble through
meadows of ego
shattered by flowers

Even satin gardenia and tropical plumeria fall
some in their perfume some while fading.

Our bushy locks thin with a smell of age
while earth receives each memory without a song.

Year after starry year we watch a rise and fall
of breath friendly talk and the look for loving.

Even our book of changes or an alchemy of illumination
all fall all into a sigh between the seeds of time.

We kiss against tomorrows but lose the chase
can't stop our coming can't forget the going.

So I surrender to minutes second by second
staying how long I hope to please the elements

And plant a fragrance of calmly working my lips
into this glorious night overspreading our watching

Our bodies with friends until we can't hold on
like falling flowers extending into wind.

Whatever your calling your sounding is plumeria
and toward the carnival of our twilight we can

At best be grace in falling and even gardenia
but slave or slave driver we must surrender as dust.

*

In good times
friends sing to me
in bad I to them

*

It all makes sense
fucking fighting
work death
daybreak starset

*

All the dawns
evening storms
lovely breasts
good talk
tickled children
blow plumeria drift

*

No stranger
to dreaming night
please razor moon
rise and save me
from this mortal dream

*

Like dying yellow flames
orange leaves feather
their way out of bright air
to the waiting earth

*

Drifting clouds
change their story
minute by minute

*

In the dew
heavy wild grass
my footprints disappear
with the morning sun

*

Blather brain
hopes fears
desire noise
glad songs
worldless dreams
the long goodbye
of waiting silence

*

Three weeks watching
my breath suddenly
think of fingering
you on your belly

*

Would I could be
who I think I am
do what I say I'll do

*

Eyes open
starlight
a meadow at dawn
a boy in the rain
eyes closed
blood of the music
the agony of bones
hopeful breath
pregnant dreams

*

On t.v. they say
pray He'll save you
from friends
turned to ash
hungry children
of unholy genocide
lonely birth

*

Death by earthquake
wedding flowers
from my fields
friends drowned
in bluer Pacific
another pink sunrise
virus killing lovers
nature's a wild motherfucker

Masturbating the Absurd

Dream: Squatting under a rotting makeshift leanto I watch tender candlelight float on the blackened shawls of pale night women shaking with habitual prayer before morning's violet horizon. One red winged blackbird slow wings through the mountain's pulse of fog hiding centuries of blue oaks. Paired moths flit near fleshy portulacaceae that thankfully overgrew last year's control burn near windowless homes off lower Mission Purisma Canyon. Laughing at his songlike shadow a ragtag bum with a patchwork coat of painted birds drags himself down Jesuita Trail. "Want to play?" His upheld arms gently invent a pale spring sky of imaginary guardian angels. We dance in Sufi circles until I'm hovering at hawk's eye view over the artful roll of lavender ceanothus hills. Ryokan grabs his beaten chest and coughs blood red clouds into the bright still air. I cover him with autumn's leaves as he gladly folds himself to sleep and dream forever in the thankful cruel earth.

*

Ryokan grew rooted in the banyan tree until flowering and invented consciousness of twilight. He surrendered to mountains of babble and joyously entered the beckoning grave with compassionate tears.

Ryokan copied his Bodhisattva poems from the breath of children the water of waters our Zen future after the cities. He chronicled poverty's lips preparing us for stones of sorrow for human dust all the while mastering light the dew drops on a lotus blossom.

Ryokan blazed crazy wisdom paths through
seasons of everyday hell becoming now my
handsome sound and recurring dream of him
handing me the glass laurel of his mouth.

Ryokan the Buddha not Buddhist getting
caught up 19 years in the brush of the brush
tucking his poems asleep until they stir
inside like mourning Ryokan the dancer
of this quiet trance patiently watching
each breath each wonderful rise and fall.

My word making
little comfort
to my bone thin
brother begging
for breath

*

Thanks night
sun earth fire
helping save
a wretch like me
a warrior of the thigh
a soldier of song

*

Quiet room
unmade bed
children playing
in the rain
stupid poems
awful silence

*

Poets are a crock
praising each the other's
bullshit me included

*

Phone quiet
t.v. off
computer silent
garden roses
so noisy
can't work

*

Yes lovers sons friends
but my poems
are my foolish gift
for someone somewhere
tomorrow and tomorrow now

*

The love of my life
pissed off
and here I sit
writing love poems

*

That black cloud
that pretty girl
feels good to sing
for them

*

Once he decided
poetry's it
she never came back

*

First music
then dance
later poesy
fucking with friends
now noisy breath

*

My poems try
your biblical soul
wet your thighs
want you
to believe
we're friends

*

Subterranean poets care
about the work of you
don't care about some of you
want to be mostly alone
wish you were always here

*

César Vallejo my mystic velvet poet whoring confessions from an ethereal gutter you trace with word shadow an immense mime of Western guilt you still winged lean Christ my beat compadre dancing me naked beyond revolutionary dark oh sublunar genius skirting emotional hopes of boyish scholar priests.

César I am your cowboy of death a hateshod fugitive driven by headline destruction blazing a trail through pandemonium where humans are eating the rivers and trees.

César I sing them your political songs of pure white narcissus mouth barbaric yawp and un-bury your man-eyes the faces of your hairy brain my dove-tame fugitive teacher I am breath-ing your future now as you take me like Dante through night flowers festered in barrio dreams two jailed poets masturbating the absurd what is the militant secret behind your exiled eyes can we help uncover the media's lips and glide beyond the wave of a wave-driving wind?

César my Amazon bird we'll fly fire-blooded singing thigh deep in the phantasmagoric self working sounds woven on the sweat loom of la raza's cry buried in sister-brotherhood we'll catch myths from a net of stars inebriate of night mouths full of smiling Dadaist surreal sequined cubist fantastic kisses César my desolate an-gel let's wing past eons of backbreaking words shoving the no longer take it into badges of dig-nified work and free play border crossing poems.

Cool March winds shake
half done same poems
off my makeshift desk
wake me from a loss dream

*

My best friend farms
worries about bugs
weeds "not the heavy shit
that's a poet's job"

*

I saw all happy stories
in God made clouds
when I was a Nowhere
West Texas kid wondering
what I'd be doing now

*

I pick silent marigolds
in the wet sunrise
shovel chicken shit
under the sweaty sun
listen for hungry poems
in the dead of night

*

Dream: armed with the *Tibetan Book of the Dead* I
hitch for Pt. Reyes but end up half drunk arguing
Marx with stoned café poets at a hip jazz bar in beat
North Beach. A poet's poet peers from an angry
streaked glass corner on bloody revolution. No
one mentions the hungry air rising around smoky
white turn-of-the-century rose-petaled Chinese
women on the painted wall next to a paisley suf-
fragette carrying a promising placard for our future.

A handsome troubadour paints a black and white
of the military industrial complex and though I'm
thinking of Mt. Diablo's future meltdown a gay
brother tattoos "now" on these very typing fin-
gers. Later we keep beat with dancing souls at the
Café of Endless Night back-grounded by red neon
streets where ebony hands offer militant prayers
to the black and blue cosmos and make their
night town angry way to a captive free Rastaman.

Would I were
a birth giver
a sister of mercy
not a bone hard
word priest sucking
the mercury air
looking for a fight
with Old Scratch easily
satisfied by the wet
power of her moan
& sleeping front to back

*

Perfect stars
give me chills
I put down
my poesy pen
who the hell
do I think I am

*

A few aching years
from now to nothing
if someone sings
the secret of my brain
felt songs of dark stars
will it have been in vain?

*

Help me hold
the lonely at graves
of fear sing
in me for the sorrow

*

Art helps some
Jesus others
but star or star fucker
the lovely rock hard
ground's always there

The Crossed Legs of Your Holy Kiss

Midsummer heat passes slowly down the thunderous Chiapas valley of conquered ghosts. Jungle fever cold sweat blears my limp eyes begging for sleep's surrendered comfort even Ecclesiastes' bony hands of blind judgment. My once and forever love carries drink from a rock covered well. Thin cows sleep nearby.

Across the dusty blessed cornfield a threadbare frightened widow holds close her naked dirty children. From the curved doorless entry to their mud hut they are sad for us.

Lightning whips around almost sweet in my half-dead brain. I keep asking about wind broken gladioli.

White fog dulls pale rainbows on dew heavy spider webs. Monkeys cackle deep in the dark Palenque jungle like sad babies in a wine given dream. In the weedy ribs of three black pyramids buttercups bear witness to white robed Mayans carrying bales of plastic on their proud ebony heads of beaten grief.

My love appears to me in the seven blowing grasses. Wild hot wind sweeps mauve tipped soft weed arms and mimes my lady's dance. She kisses my hands of grief helps me forget the garlands of death my brother's helpless tears.

> Our woven hands &
> beating breasts
> hold holy dear
> our laughing vows
> like little blood brothers

*

My silent confession awakes on the hot crucifix of
secret breath between the crossed legs of your holy
kiss. My sorrow was sweet Jesus or Buddha cry-
ing on good Friday was my brainy balls of manna
and fingered rosary of books and nardos until you
prayed for my flowering and sang in my seeded
marrow as I ascended in the virgin of you stark
naked sucking the spent lips of your satisfied sleep.

Bold young and girlish thin
in her handmade summer
dress of desire shimmering
in the laughing moon's
rhythm of lover's light

*

Watching with righteous love
eternal light fall through our
future children's
Ethiopian generations
Latin fingers & American lips

*

Hot and bothered
pulled over
on a midnight street
fingering sucking
under a flood of stars
who cares what
the t.v. neighbors think

*

Joined at the groin
deep breathing
our bodied origins
signing spiritual yeses

through centuries of tears
after there's birthing you
& the good book tree of me
there's bodiless meeting
in the imagination of heaven

*

When I am no longer
a ring on your hand
a song in your sorrow
I am gone

*

When you hurt
my love turns soldier
against all biblical stones
I'd even marry death
if hurled toward you

*

I remember and forget
my New Year's resolutions
when she tipsy slips
out of her sheen and satin
'round 'bout midnight

*

A certified fool
for the bedlam of love
I'd fight the very heart
of endless night
to bring you light

*

'til death do us part
I'll remember tearful you
making intellectual fun
of a summer cloud

*

Give me your cock
kiss yes give
your soul yes
your prisoned heat
now leave me
the Catholic Eve
you the Jew Adam

*

You rage I'm
a selfish bastard
penniless poet
lazy dreamer
but I'm in what
some call love
with the gardenia of you
God knows I'll never leave
even when with Him

*

You film bluebells
swaying under bluebirds
circling under blue backed clouds
swirling in the big blue
beyond blue I lounge
in blue grass singing
the blues waiting for blue
rain the blue winged bee
your blue blue eyes

*

Gently I pinched
her nipples gladly
gave her head
on the hood
of someone's sports car
her cell ringing ringing

*

I surrender
to her naked poet's
breath it's lust
I guess but
I'm grave robbing
happy singing inside
the heaven of her

*

After her exquisite flowering
& my strut & wondering
I godless worry
about the cradle to cradle

*

She lives in quiet
with precious flowers
on the expensive hill
me with my cars & parts
in the singing barrio
God is great

*

I probably kiss
to hear the deep
the tongue of you
weeping with laughter

*

In the drop dead
of crippling night
cock felt vows
painted with whispers
prayers & candlelit legs
we'll forget

Against the Living Air

Our friendly sister's body ashes scatter in the zodiac of celestial wind blowing off kind Pacifico across the forgiving earth she planted each dead spring into every summer forgetting her birth home brewed pregnant fears conceived down the road from Jefferson's righteous denial to forgive his blood Blacks prayed for under the Samson stick those righteous beatings dearly given on the altar of righteous intentions by her proper father's rope of hate thanking Jesus for his privilege of her first breath.

Under the safe hip California sky our only God fearing friend (in my crying brain) romanced freed thoughts at her home grown dinners of intellectual tears for frequent guests those rare bourgeoisie nights after breathless felt talk of the warming air's future her Southern drawl and cautious laughter gone now only these fucking ashes falling about us hoping she's forever found quiet eternally safe now while we earthheld remember her love for the cool lavender winds of safe Provence the blooming blue Santa Barbara manzanita the handsome geese honking sky of homophobic green Virginia.

We're all waiting breathful with the dried veins of her brutal voice all saved in our scattered memories safe in this night song (she asked me to close her eyes after death) in this breathing handsake reaching in vain for her safe hello our gone good friend gone for good safe with Chagall's bearded Creator who birthed us all screaming all safe.

> A sundancing butterfly
> in summer wind
> vanishes into the light

*

The old fashion names
of a husband and wife
side by side in the ground

*

Given names make us real
words near birth breathed
from fond mouths later
unhappily surrendered
to stonecutter strangers

*

What's a creature
'spose to do
sickly children
crying friends
stuck in a cloud
shadowed body
of future earth meat

*

Early spring
a flock of sparrows
returns to his weed
breezy grave

*

All the dawns
evening storms
lovely eyes
good talk
tickled children
blow jacaranda drift

*

Weed roots weave
through remembered friends
their sucker love poems
sadly forgotten
good hard work
mostly unread

*

My best friend's grave
she loved soul singing
my naughty sons asleep
now she's the wind's
melody of bending grass

*

Watching the life giving sun
set God fearing she thanked
me on her foul death bed
for washing her tired feet

*

An invisible loon sings
under graying skies
I scatter my 2nd best friend's
ashes on the dirty black
lake of broken winter reeds

*

She's dead
even so
even so
thought I saw
her laughing today

*

The lost eyes told me
that I'd play catch
with his lost sons
long time after
he thought breathed

*

The god forsaken sun falls through light holes
in the windy barrio afterrain. A mangy dog
paws at an unmarked grave.

Our small gathering stands together with folded
Catholic hands. One small voice mutters from
a gilded book of hope. Rain runs black from
inside unread names hand cut in cold marble.

A little girl plays with her reflection in the asphalt rain
blowing bougainvillea cling to her bright raincoat.

After first breath
crying laughter
sex money kids
artful musical prayer
after last breath

*

Hopeful surfers fade into siren shadows of the
going down sun flattened on the channel's red
horizon. The swollen thunder at Rincon breaks
and drowns hysterical sobs of the dark woman
bent over her long hair lover.

Oh Dion only yesterday we listened for the
future in the handsome wind of your wife's truck
garden near the happy banana trees.

Your ocean strength sways in your bowed sunflower field. At sunset windfalls appears in light prisms and shake off a death dancing perfect moth caught forever in a waving phosphorescent old star spider's web.

I can still hear you singing carefree to violent waves. We were young invulnerable.

Laughing boys teasing
their barking dogs
help me work and forget
the worm happy dust

*

If we could come back
her a book of flowers
our boys blades of grass
me the invisible wind

*

Quivering thighs
a child's song
bullshit poets
movie magic good
to be above ground

*

When I'm memories
my kids will think of me
when they're long gone
I've only a poem or two

*

Some say truth & art
helps some Allah others
but star or star fucker
the rock hard ground
is always there

*

Friendly talk at a friend's wake
big houses fast cars who's hot
I smile cry what else

*

The storm driven sea
blows my brother's ashes
back into my thinking

*

Against the living air lapping under the newly risen
east cradled moon grass blades blow back through my
crouched shadow over your luminous grave drowned in
my blood hugging ceremony of roses pining in you still.

(Roaring a river from your soft breast your unsung
throat calls my hearty father your body's husband
deep screams of distant nights spread legged your
flowering mother thighs rocking open as you taste
him with your wet eyes and breath sown wishes).

My birth gave you a man child standing over your
melted flesh maggots milking at your brain. I have
wandered from you yet always return oh earth held
beginning. Like an old man's desire to see home
again I pass the locked door of your flowing hair
pressed in the eagle arms of master him that made
me in you the night of she bear in the starry cloister
of Virgo—by the handle he dips the spike of grain
breaking the soon forgotten woman from whom I'm

Scrubbing mother's
gravestone black
with L.A.'s soot
this winter of regrets

*

Married at 15
4 kids by 20
angry as hell
unschooled she
cried when she beat
us for our own good
sad to think of her
the funhouse fat lady alive

*

My first love
died today
the wisteria
hanging over her
back yard fence
hurts me

*

Winter wind whistles
about gravestones
one by one by one
spirits away
her favorite French violets

*

Her ashes of skin & bone
drift on the calmed lake
of sirens in this felt poem
of night after night
we remember her by

*

A widower's warm breath
fogs the cracked window
all day the wash whipped
by cold rain

Of Her I Sing

In mind flashes you stoke my late night tears
as the last season of our musical sex moans in
the cat crying night. Your calling song wakes
me from workaday video with the harp of your
silk voice making the birth of morning sway
your secret rage of giving and sexual take.

Your rivering siren flows in macho me against
the slain metropolis and Judas bomb that your
underground mention changes to tender hope
and wonderful rage against my felony of pos-
session the get-you got-you you massage with
treaty signed legs warming my professional solitude.

I mindfully carry our war music into jazzed para-
noia our dissonant arms of tender hope. Your
tongue lines my lips with a hip Torah of grace.
I lick your turned over ass as all day and night
stress and blind nods become an open meadow
of gloriosa and your single good night kiss.

> With your spiritual leash
> of never and always
> you pull the flesh of me
> gladly weeping into the infinite
> grave of the everyday world

> *

> Perfectly still
> she listens to falling
> cherry blossom music
> the mournful summer sky
> and I seldom envious
> a god seeking witness

to the brutal rhythms
of quiet evening
in her silhouette

*

Couldn't remember
where I parked
I was lonely thinking
of you your candlelit
door slightly open

*

Skin to skin
& the blossoms
of your whisper
closer come closer
my darling we're
on our way to where
we've never been

*

The stained glass
of your morning
eyes the rosary
of your proverbial voice
there is a God

*

Rocking you open
I thought about dying
not waking the baby

*

The good and bad
years on your face
don't matter my love

you're still moist
to my boyish fingers
kind to my lost soul

*

Had to hit the lupine
lined road & zen sit
under noisy redwoods
too bad I keep thinking
of you making green tea

*

Cock tears
wish you
poems kids
with you feverish
with you broke
everything

*

Stroking her ass
while she fingers
herself I listen
to her breathing
watch the candles
burn the night

*

Of course of her I
man that I am sing
freely when she shares
the awful truth of her
promised eyes and
on rare satisfied nights
her secret living music

*

She cried
as I wiped
vomit off
her party dress

*

I love she comes
goes whenever
calls talks philosophy
while I'm bone silent
in the body of print heaven
forgotten my impossible dreams
lost among the living shadows
of my unimportant daily opera

Lost and Found in the Newly Risen Dark

Late sunrays fall across the bony pink under wings of hunting pelicans that trace in prehistoric airwaves the sculpted Pt. Reyes seashore cliffs. Splendid Jupiter glows beyond Wildcat Beach just above late August Saturn. Western bluebirds sync with the molten sun in square miles of dappled mirrors shaking into nothing at all. Waves form waves and vanish like so many important faces into the ever same ocean.

My eartheld sister's spirit her kind face wades into an emptying stream. Her ballet fingers perform an out-blossoming wild lily mudra while she calmly charms the Buddha and tiptoe steps into the same river twice. Her grateful lover my found brother sits at water's edge watching a redtail updraft as he forgets his wife's cancer and changes into a brown bank of waving thistles.

I smile with them on Pelican Pt. My empty thought turns to our earlier trail where white deer lounged in forget-me-nots. The pine's green voice mirrors sacred places—wish I knew how to get there. My unmasked face in the backcountry spring—no that wasn't me. No matter how many poems, still prefer the coast's violet veined wild iris. Night sounds hint and fade as even now we are lost and found in the newly risen dark.

> One more drink
> and my best friends
> have all the answers
> even for death

*

Bay laurel sycamore elms
delirious winds singing above
a cast of woman made
children hiking to Crystal Lake

*

A sometime friend married after a light rain to-
day on the cusp of Capricorn under the blessed
influence of modern love. Delicate Venus hung
sincerely in the brutal changing priestly twilight.

"Unlearn and perfect Christ the wing of a dove
in flight" Father Dario preached. "Love like red-
woods giving light and space and explore the
generous dance of wedding trust in yourself in God."

Inside the sheltered corner of the over-flowered
chapel believing everything & nothing I broke
thoughts about the air as cancer and romanti-
cally became a slight part of their jazzy high in
the Jesus crotch of blind faith and signing hands
crossed in prayer freely given their savage holy bliss.

Outside plumb blossoms folded on the wait-
ing ground while their imaginary chalice of
kneaded belief lowered their real world pride
as they gladly drank the operatic body of heav-
enly songs rejoicing the reckoned passage.

At rest they centered as lying down animals not
chest beating beasts but fiery brain above starry heart
below. With 100,000 bows & without thinking they
entered a perfect music smoking the palace of the
other dancing the Sufi planets their heavenly sirens
praising the luminous sleep of their found child.

You'd think after all
the struggling years
of watching breath
and mindful chanting
I'd know something
besides the violent cry of birth
the miracle of a woman's body
her spiritual gift her lovely death

*

Why lock myself away
in zazen unthinking
unangry unsad
occasionally imagining
yr wonderful face
I'd rather kiss you
here there & now

*

One God many stories
holding you the kids
walking the blue earth
singing away the pain
with friends on the road
what more

*

Always blaming everyone
I'll try but never change
the sorrow of handsome
night where lovers cheating death
bow forever now and then

*

I walk quickly by
the sidewalk beggar
the subway stabbing
who the hell
do I think I am

*

The face I face
is not the one
I think I am

*

Dear Lobo:

A van full of Aquarius children picked me
up shivering near thin scrub oaks comforted
by little sparrows barely surviving the U.S.
101 yesterday. A coffee shop newspaper
confirmed my first hysterical glimpse of gray
brown San Fernando Valley a thick can-
cerous air unhealthful for all living things.

With an eye on twilight we must fight money lend-
ers people users lying through the heart hollow
unhappy bureaucrats. Forget this-want-that
and conjure god awfully a let go of ego cry to
dematerialize. Why can't we labor love and tran-
scend our aboriginal exiled-from-gov't. mind?

Oh to tumble wavelength headlong as warriors of hope even to stoke the warmed crease of an earth-lover's song instead of casting our vain prayers to great mountains betrayed by superhighways excommunicated by gold churches of American progress.

> With a hand in thought,
> Genaro

> Under the Coke sign
> bloodlike graffiti cries
> "eat less 'til all
> eat as much"

> *

> "Look at you look at me
> love trust all that jazz
> think Jesus'll 'cover us
> with leaves & a blanket
> from the moon?'"

Sorrowful Months of Unusual Rain

Sorrowful months of unusual rain stunt fluffy rainbow asters sowed under last cool March's invisible sadness. Listening to broken hearted arias my some time lover stares at leaning cut plum blossoms. On the underground radio hopeless voices report uncovered mass graves of pure Huehuetenango's slaughtered children.

Spittle bug suck at delicate stems of dainty wall-flowers companion planted with hoped for pearly tuberoses. Hoeing muddy weeds a street weary oldtimer passes by: "Lucky to work in a garden."

Streamside our borrowed flower field common crow watch us plant Aztec zinnias just before the red Toltec sun comes down. The talking windbreak eucalyptus sway in the lazy breeze scattered radioactive air from innocent cracked canisters in transit through the nearby Mediterranean styled airport.

I wander down rows of baby's breath avoiding husks of dead caterpillars. Yesterday spread the last volunteered ranunculas on my surrendered good friend the poet's beat grave remembering a rainy Buddhist Xmas he was gladly writing pious love poems.

> The summer garden
> feeds us with flowers
> until playing worms
> and winter earth turn us
> to mourned souls

*

Impatient for irises
to green up
would old I could
be so blue pretty
young spring
after finally spring

*

Forgot about street
lined jacaranda
until they bloomed
perfect again this year

*

Pruned fed waited
months for my hybrid roses
broken petals windy rain

*

Why praise the precious
earth those six feet
under stopped
singing long ago

*

The science of
mystical seeds
restores your left brain
faith in everyday
miracles like noisy
children the music
of old trees

*

Picking organic cotton
in a fever driven dream
our Lady of Guadalupe
gives her nardos
to push on

*

For a million dollar
view of bluer Pacifico
mustard seed dangle
dangerously over Highway 1

*

If only my flowers
grew themselves
I'd daydream
I'd time to write
more poems daybreak
to night while farming
my darkness

*

He worries nights
about rotting unsplit
tubers the blue heron
who watched over
their proud dirt
before the bank
took their years
the family farm

*

Helpless I listen
breathe deeper
as late windy
showers lay
down our giant dahlias

*

Before the fall
rains planted
weeded fed weeded
our bearded iris weeded
again in early spring
then patient gophers
ate them silvered
leaves and all

*

While she arranges
roses she speaks
with hidden pain
about her beautiful God
her hard husband
the endless war

*

The average farmer fights
wind loves hates elemental
rain seasons of heat
God's plan for pests
worships fearful in the dark
as old earth turns
all before another sun sets

*

Planted all day
cooked dinner
bathed the kids
paid bills read
watched her breathing
rolled over slept

*

Early santanas
burn spring's
waving grasses
then bring out
the playing voices of girls
dogs and their boys

*

One wife two boys
not enough friends
for years I gladly
listened to my old
4-H banana tree
broken now
by last night's
unwelcomed storm

*

Amazing how seed
earth water
and horseshit
become a flower
lifting a woman's skirt

*

6 to 6 deep plowing
then wall-to-wall
screaming kids
a leaky roof
the old tractor
my darling one
notebooks full
of dreams
this is it

*

Pissed off
then laughing
at my dancing weeds
always coming
back singing to me
no matter what
tune I play

*

My noisy flowers
sing for fiery romance
chilly fuckups
prom get luckies
the bride and groom
the rented room widower
one day they'll sing
above me & you

The Turquoise Mockingbird of Light

Dreams: *the still unborn one inside after cold sweating her last breath wishing for birds of paradise. Wet black hair covers her bone white face.*

Weary midwives cry rubbing her cool blue hands in the oil of snakes & dress her limp pelvis for her lost lover to bear on the stone cross of his beaten back into the breaking twilight.

Streams of crickets stop as they pass.

> Making love
> to make babies
> I kiss your eyes
> as if God
> were inside you

*

The blue-eyed gypsy speaks my pregnant one with her jaguar like night grace. Like birds-into-air petals of her glide all around inside the dream of me.

"I've tasted your hot seed and a soft light entered us like a dream of loins. Ah your milky groans dark to dawn steeped in our waving hips until we unfolded as drunken velvet gardenias.

The cold high plains swell with fields of bulbous iris. Soon their bearded fire will sway in a flower laden wind.

May we bring our gentle seed into blood. May the four corners bless our breath and the birth of spring."

*

Flies make lazy circles around the braided heads of chatting pregnant Lacadonians. They drink lemon weed tea near cut sunflowers and swap fears about their uncome babies. Dazed by dysentery my love-with-child her long face of dread listens as she fingers her black neck beads in the warmed corner of the shaded midwife's porch.

"Some say you can't look at the dead by hanging or his cord turns him blue."

"May it never happen."

"If you yearn at the half-shadowed sun his lips tear. So put cold obsidian to your swelling breasts. If you walk out starless nights you'll fall. His groin swells welt blood runs down his screaming legs."

"So many sleepless bird still night."

"And keep your macho half-ocelot lover curved night long with a soft penis near your silk side!"

"I'm not a magic womb queen or some mortality goddess though once I saw the swollen earth buckle in late summer hot rocks in the black air. You must cut yourself from the stark tree of everyday wrath or your twisted fear opens growths on his warrior back. I pray for you and all ladies each child all precious souls. With these hands in thought I see the miracle that's your son's first dawn."

*

The fragrant night before we bathe in summer's waters and sleep until morning turns rose. In the hot reed house she howls squats water rages from her splashing vulva. Steam hisses.

I give her rosemary tea and sweep the waiting house as she screams.

Many cries many. Acacias brush away the stars night golden they wave shadows over her sloped belly a hill rise beneath her generations of Eve.

On the time worn altar of utter woman she is the vein of her pain her morphed face all tears all fours pawing the prehistoric floor. Evolutionary fear in her here now eyes like a frightened deer her quick breath veils wild nights aflame with the wild gleam of our wish that opened her calligraphy of love.

Her bent knees press her swelling breasts wind leaves like the lion-in-man pose. Crying out for a child! Push push grunting breathe breathe air air earth earth fire fire scream scream. Mist.

My helpless tears fall ancient stars in her deep galaxy sighs birth fluid oozes birth blood cries. Yes. A blessed haze and more natural aches grunts push push bending the sacred womb. Transformed I catch the holy body. Yes. A hairy skull his sad eyes yes his pained mouth yes fire breathing throat crying yes our body child. Yes. Yes.

Suckling sweet nipple milk her smile my face: his.

*

The wrinkled one with hands of life breathed over the still water touched it to the child's lips.

"Descend into the blue river of suffering my turquoise mocking bird of light. You come from your mother's soft womb with a dark hunger for return to earth our bed of flowers and death. After shouldering all the tears you'll touch the ground. Let it bless you as you yield and finally you too are wild grass."

Our biblical son
keeps us up all night
cries for his natural mama
good I caught him
heard his first cry
'cause I'm naturally happy
cleaning shit off his ass

*

Forget poetry
going out jazzed
our winter born boy needs
his diaper changed
her ancient tit
me house cleaning
singing lullabies like a dove

*

She gave birth
to our sons
on the floor
of the house I built
that's the unrivalled it
the bread of art maybe
the sunlit hills in paradise

*

I slip into my son's room
just to make sure
he's breathing

When Night Rises

Looking out on the sun stained garden's Olmec stone face ole Grandpa Joe visualizes the Latin southpaw's screwball once again as he pours one more imported tequila near the orange Thanksgiving full moon spreading its teardrop light through the crystal prism hanging in the southeast facing dining room window.

Sneaking behind him my future blood son finger scoops whipped cream off the warm afternoon cooling pumpkin pie side-by-side the neighbor's gift of hot tamales. He smells like eucalyptus out back where he lost his best baseball.

Escaped from my personal gallery of doubt I'm on new age duty in the steamed up kitchen cutting veggies eavesdropping on friends' heated talk about the right and left graves of the Third World and now as the sorry time for Revelations' apocalyptic moon of blood.

My wonderful love with her ribbon-braided hair leans her perfumed neck near Jesus' hand thrown vase of floating lilies. Surrendering she listens patiently to her Catholic mother with her brought-along apron complain about the loose legged sins of a free love cousin.

Sleeping dogs lie near my hastily invited passed out compadre in front of the downstairs den t.v. football game. Down the one way road old people stare at their holiday food in the recessed light of a muzak coffee shop.

Near our front porch overgrown passion flower vine a chalice of Oaxacan spliff rises past an overweight friend chanting Hare Hare into the leafy street full of family talk and the unforgettable harvest moon.

My son says grace
we eat argue
war worry together
& in the blessed
presence of bending callas
I'm thankful

*

A circle completes
when my roundabout
words enter the intelligent
mouths of my sons'
open struggle
for the happy go lucky
journey of their sad glad lives

*

Late afternoon October
fall sycamore shadows
blowing elms the kite flying
laughter of sons their dogs me

*

I want to kiss
you darling
as you worry
out loud about
the women
of Darfur
take bread
from the oven
call friends
to come
and get it

*

Children reach
for falling snow
trampling veined leaves
with footloose laughter
fearless of winter's night
the certain bones

*

Worried about mother
rats eating the wallboard
in the dead of night
I get up cover the children

*

3 a.m. dragged my boys
up the mountain
to watch the meteor shower
sons and fathers
everywhere I hope

*

For a proud moment
walking downtown
buying school clothes
my teenage son held
my aging hand

*

In his 2nd grade
crayon portrait
my 2nd boy glad day ready
his Godloving mom hugging him
big curious brother ready to hit it
me head in a clouds of words
with our smiling Zen cat

*

Argued with my prodigal sons
the light in their voices
the silent stones of their tears
explained the burden of rules
they still do what they please

*

In the back seat
good boys brag
about good girls
what they wanna
do with them

*

Thankful he came home
his boys hold their breath
until they hear him snoring

*

She pulled
my pants down
while I ironed
said it turned her on

*

Angry lover
shadowed by debts
demanding cats
old house
not what I
imagined being
the other

*

I can't get
the boys to come in
from the spring rain

*

Teasing school kids
vanish in a fall shroud
of fog laughing laughing

*

Sling shot boys
kick red and gold leaves
swirling down the street
of locked doors
at the happy end
of Indian summer

*

When the stone
of night rises
I a thief of songs
yearn for the music
of a woman's love &
when my out the door
sons sneak one by one
late back home
I breathe deep again

*

My 1st son's dream: *God was swimming in a sea full of stars at night. He flew down into the waves crashing like thunder. Dad you stared into his eye. His breath was warm. You opened your eyes inside him. I jumped into you.*

We were like daffodils.

The streams were noisy with fish.

You washed my feet and we breathed with our face at
the sea covered with moon. It sounded like snow until a
rainbow in the mist broke like air bubbles in your beard
in His beard too—the beard you wear all your lives.

We heard the sounds everything is.

Then a woman came into us like God. We named all
the animals until the flowers became trees. He told us
stories of when he was me running naked through the
sands and picnics. Someone was playing music by a fire.
I remember the kisses mother wept when I was born.

A Half Painted House

Squatting near her bed of double ranunculas my better half cried endlessly this heavy morning of our heartfelt change going now on a second summer of not much talk. Wrapping her perfect anger inside she pulled her woven thoughts of nevermore over her turned away forehead of grief those dark pinched lips after our last fight.

Up from the Baja's heat tropical showers slapped at California lupine and lay down late summer's grasses against the cracked Chumash mountains. Mute hours after days fighting burnt out and pissed off by the all day electric nagging and biting my teeth I hiked into the hammer of summer the Los Padres back country mile into mile until a rattlesnake hunter stopped me into why not drunkenness. Sad arms folded I rested like a scolded dog waited in the breathing chaparral light for the beating wings of sandstone swallows. A red-tail hawk circled over the curved manzanita canyon. Sitting through the hot rain we passed yarns and apparent wisdom until sleep my tequila skull dreaming her favorite smells.

> Dead broke
> dead flowers
> a half painted house
> what the hell drunk
> with another bum
> & the autumn wind

> *

> An old friend
> "Sure there's Gods
> brats buddies

honky tonk song
but wiser at 50
in these blue mountains
I prefer going home
with a good woman"

*

After soul fighting
all labored night
bruising the religious
grief of our married soul
the matter of fact sun rises
as she brushes me
out of her tangled hair
and I go away blinded
by her song of sorrow

*

Barely here her
republican eyes
on summer white clouds
as I paint her drugstore nails
listen to her glamour & skin

*

Blood angry I didn't
notice her new dress
I was stupid busy
watching her bridal legs
sway the Chinese silk

*

Dear One:

In this raining metropolis haze hip women pass
through me anointed with your gossamer cloud
grace. Your wet dirty love tosses in hot memory

of yr heaven felt parted thighs of happy light.
Behind my zithered whine and vacant liquor eyes
I'm writhing for you under winter's torn skies.

The rainy stars fade in the lonely cold morning.

A managed kiss in thought.

Lobo

      Gray and white
      thunder clouds
      a keepsake
      of her stone-
      like face

          *

      Kept wanting
      more kisses
      then sex sleeping
      curled like cats
      at daybreak
      she wanted out

          *

Endless days and crying moons leave their dusty
signature on the glass jar holding your withered
freesias. Off wet silvered asphalt soft thought
light shimmers a glimpse of your ghostly frown
and bar drugged stagger down on me with your
long pointed finger of guilt.

After wine sick days and awake nights the
thinning rain reflects our angry memory: you up a
red slick alley clown miming sad kisses heckling
me from the angry distance.

In this drizzle before the honor of light your
secret faces flash tears and ecstasy. Under my
brown snake thighs your windy fire pulse flowers.
I sweat hold you savage sucking your angry lust.

I should've
looked longer
when you left
angry a plumeria
in your hair

*

Nobody told me
to love her secrets
even I the fool for love knew
she'd the empress of soul
leave this life or after

*

Half you half me
our kids didn't know
where to go when
she moved out

*

Memory of bitter light hides behind Berkeley's
swollen rain clouds. Sulfur crime street lamps
bleed unreal nightfall across our emptied bed
of broken you bitching out your fever of right.

Your give me skin left voices in me ripple still.
I vowed to break bread with your gentle hands
open hearts of your poetry with a forever ring. You
definitely promised to make me sing my senses
but my shadow faces night blind over ego pools.

I cannot own you only remember thyself to paper
song.

In my daypack
lily of the valley
weaves through
the boulevard crowd
to our empty room

*

Early winter light
failed as we watched
the unkind years
on each other's face

*

Our unmarried eyes drift
anywhere everywhere but
upon the hidden other
wasting our promised tongues
forsaking our forgotten dreams

*

Obscene vacant
hellos lies
about painful trivia
oh my lost
& once forever love

*

Fool I am
not to have
kissed her joy
soon enough
I'll be flies' food

Gone that hopeful kiss that placed our breath to
stone seed beneath the garden of our heart and
the window of night.

Gone our lovely lick after lick near the wild blue
delphiniums beyond gone now your cock's head kiss
quivering like streams in late spring the windy gold
in the pregnant treetops above our natural bed.

Gone that good gone kiss of talk and covering
the children asleep gone that final god damn
night screaming "I hate yr feel yr dreamed
myth of immortality by words yr manly logical
criticisms" chanting at the top of your voiced
miracle of venom "Sterile dumb aieeeeeee!"

Gone stroke after stroke of your deep woman hips
gone your kiss of bread wronged kiss this bleeding
kiss of screamed twilight breathless I'm putting out.

> All her orifices
> closed that awful
> morning of angry
> finding out

> *

> Cried you
> a thousand songs
> never forget I
> breathed you

> *

> Ashamed I waited
> 'til the end of night outside
> your lover's expensive house
> the angry wind blowing
> through what's left of me

*

I was
okay until
morning doves
started cooing
at each other

*

Night fog covers
wishful lovers'
dark hush
silences night birds
everything but
my longing breath of you

*

Hope woke
when the door
creaked open
but it was her cat
come in
from a night
of love making

*

Down on
my knees
asking God Buddha
Jake the Snake
help me stop
imagining her

*

God damn
mosquito it's bad
enough she's god
knows where tonight

*

He hated her
lover lied
prayed forgave
to bring her back

*

Wanted her
good looks
kids song
long life until
death takes
her garden of flesh
& plenty of sorrows
now what

*

Dear Lobo:

Pity your hot headed mournful penis death by your manmade woman field you so lovingly sowed brother.

I wonder a brainy mouthful about priorities and ponder your Dantesque lady worship. Can't you let go of male ego at the throat of patriarchal romance your curved rush into her dark panther and the fantasy smell of her every after in your later-in-the-day slow fingered pussy stroke of pleasant beard? That's all turned in civilization's commercial tongue into a raving celestial goddess doll and you a cock-whipped swan of magazine sex. Can't you trash and transcend that Western implosion?

The real work is our tongue of massage on lips of evolution words as the hands of love carried with the labor of flowers becoming a many thousand petaled song fist. Let's cross ourselves with humankind & hand-in-hand

hard work against a chemical earth. Kisses.
Your brother,

Genaro

Naked's not
enough she
wanted a God
window to my soul
the proud language
of my secret poems

*

Dancing in cities
quiet in the redwoods
I wander worry wish
and unwish carry on
with a lock of her hair

*

The fire burns
low as I run
out of wine words
then she calls
asks if she can
come over

*

Years chasing
a lively skirt
head in books
money worries
now sleeping with
my good old dog
late nights waiting
for the phone
to please ring

*

Something about
skin to skin
the music of wine
as we danced dance
almost had it
but like a favorite dream
nothing here or there

*

Tried loving her
for years dumb
thinking the breath
of words & the romance
of tears could heal
the stupid fury of my soul

*

Figures the watch
she gave me
stopped and
there's a leak
in the roof above
our wedding bed

*

I don't get it
gone children
lost loves
sick friends
joyless graying
unkissed
pissing blood

*

Lived lost
in a cage
of ego
tried to
make her
dance happy
thought we
would run
forever fearless
with wolves

*

All the song licking
& belly laughter
couldn't stop
the angry night
sadness of a failing star

*

Keep thinking
there's something
someone somewhere's
gonna save me

*

The winter wind
comes up with your
miracle voice of faith
in the dappled laurels
the way you
used to sing

*

Gladly gave her
my seed my poems
a song of laughter
all my hard

squirreled dinero
held her against
stolen afternoons
waited until she came
again and lovely
again wild

*

Happy just yesterday
surrounded now
by the silent grief
of our long goodbye

*

The star find my spirit sought drowned in
hate fissures your holiday mind knew sad
sack me clothed in wishes when I giddy
passed through you rakehellied in precious
thought as we dressed and undressed our
yes and wink of shy stares and wonder.

You ate my mind's flesh inside the whine we
gladly bitched out the patriarch your screams
blistered with feminist tears lit the scalded air
and your give me Ester skin plucked empty piths
pulled through our throwaway Broadway kisses.

Blinded by windy
thighs and moist whispers
I bought her purse
of sorrow for a come
get me smile

*

In the narcissus
of dreams
I hold
my breath
for your steps
until the hills
turn green

*

Thought we
were in it
together but
you went
your liberated way
though my every pore
opened for
the smile of you

*

In the end
a cheek kiss
half a smile
her car fading
into the long
foolish night
the waning moon

*

Night long talks
joyous sleep
after years
of pleasure
sitting now

wordless
mindless
breathing out
illusions
of our past

*

Like Christ's
regrets on the terrible
cross of unknowing
God blue I long
for your sacred you

*

Watching you leave
in the moonlit wind
you want me back?

An Angry Kiss

Rickshaw diesel air rises above a junk field as I pass down the fly ruled streets hoping for an apple. A flower vendor sings to the swarming bees in the sticky Asian afternoon. Everyone is calm. A young bodhisattva smokes a quiet cigarette in the rusted backseat of his waiting bus.

Scrounging for food behind a foreign restaurant barefoot a small bronze woman holds tight her baby pulling at the silk scarf woven in her silk black hair. With a terrible grin she calls me "Joe" and blows an angry kiss off the tip of her bruised hand.

High above bi-colored eight-sided happy kites are mastered by tireless children running along the left thigh of the sleeping golden Buddha.

> A sidewalk vendor
> plays make-believe
> with his crippled boy
> in front of the cinema

*

On the hot road to Lumbini a teenage mother weeps. Her swell-bellied child whines for the milk of her sad breasts. On the rusty floor of the overpacked bus she tries to sleep sitting up. Her tired licefull head rests on my denim shoulder of embroidered flowers. Humid afternoon dusty light hours before our stop.

We pass roadside lotus floating in circles within circles beneath stone face gods. Up a dirt road a sickly girl pisses on her wounded feet. Sweat fans out through saffron robes of monks arguing about tolerance.

On the endless road
swatting God's mosquitoes
another everyday
miracle sunset

*

Years wondering
about where is God
loving better women
talking with now and then friends
playing with the real of children
planting loving flowers
breathing forgotten words

*

After the long thunder and lightning night even the roosters sleep through dawn. Rag clothed silent village children scavenge our garbage and steal my pens. Faking sleep I love them. Still sore from the all day after day climb down and up centuries of caravan trails to Tatapani's baths and then promised Tibet.

Blowing sleet yesterday. Rested in the afternoon warmth of a stone tea shop met by many smiles covered with mud in my funny uncombed beard.

Near Ulleri women draped in saris bathed gossiping about a hooka smoker waiting on the hillside staring at watery Anapurna floating on the glass rice fields.

My brother presses petunias for his lover's satisfaction. A smallpoxed girl turns to him pleading "Namaste, please eat them." Handing me an English school book laughing kids beg for stories.

After a hard day's hike
a stray dog and I
scratch in the welcomed sun

*

Awakened by red feathered mules mak-
ing long ago sounds with their Tibetan bells
down the sleeping valleys of smoke. Squatted
before Anapurna coughing up mucus.

Down the solemn
trail slate butterflies
float like drifting leaves

*

Near Ghorapani miniature calendulas and
screamin children make me forget as they play
imaginary balls in a pasture.

On the move for many years my heaviest pack still
my weary ego. After trekking for raining weeks
too sick and tired to pick leeches off my legs. The
damn flies are so happy just to sun dance around
my sleepy head.

Painting her nails
a pretty English woman
dangles her feet
over a 1,000 foot cliff

*

Camped near the Inn of the Beginning next to a hillside
stuppa that holds the ashes of the village widower's
only child. My tired faithful brother snores in his
full moon misty golden beard. He fell asleep talking
about statue-like rice farmers watching snow slides
while white monkeys cackled from a bamboo grove.

Wake from a bad dream
in the late moonlight fallen
on absolutely Machupuchare

*

A fat old woman
rocks on her porch
smoking a lonely cigarette

*

Lovers laugh
in the friendly distance
18,000 miles away
I moan in the silvered equinox
for my love my life

*

Her pressed violets
fall from my daybook
as I write about her

Screenwriter, farmer, poet, critic, translator, film maker, director, producer, teacher—Paul Lobo Portugés is the author of *Saving, Grace, Hands Across the Earth, The Visionary Poetics of Allen Ginsberg, Aztec Birth, Paper Song,* and *The Flower Vendor.* He has received awards from the Fulbright Commission, the Ford Foundation, the National Endowment, the UC Regents, the Focus Foundation, and the Briarcomb Foundation. At present, he is a Film Studies& Media Lecturer at the University of California, Santa Barbara.

Printed in the United States
200439BV00001B/214-219/A